MW01711663

# Saturday People

# And

# Other Poems

**By R.J. Lever**

**and**

**Diane Lee**

**Illustrations by Mitch Lee**

Printed by Endeavor Books
A division of Mountain States Lithographing
133 S. McKinley Street, Casper, Wyoming 82601-2744

Second printing

Printed in the United States of America



International Standard Book Number: 978-1-4507-0457-1

# Table of Contents

# Saturday People

Saturday people invariably
sleep in later than they really should.

And Saturday people
often drive sixty
miles to that optional
sporting event they just have to see.

Saturday people still believe they really can
be friends with that last wife
and that first love still can be revived.

Saturday people, unfortunately,
procrastinate too long,
dream much too much,
and sometimes imagine they've done
what they've only thought about.

Saturday people fancy
themselves younger than they
really are,
fantasize about big breaks,
wealth and fame, and about
living free.

Saturday people would
probably threaten you and me.

R.J. Lever

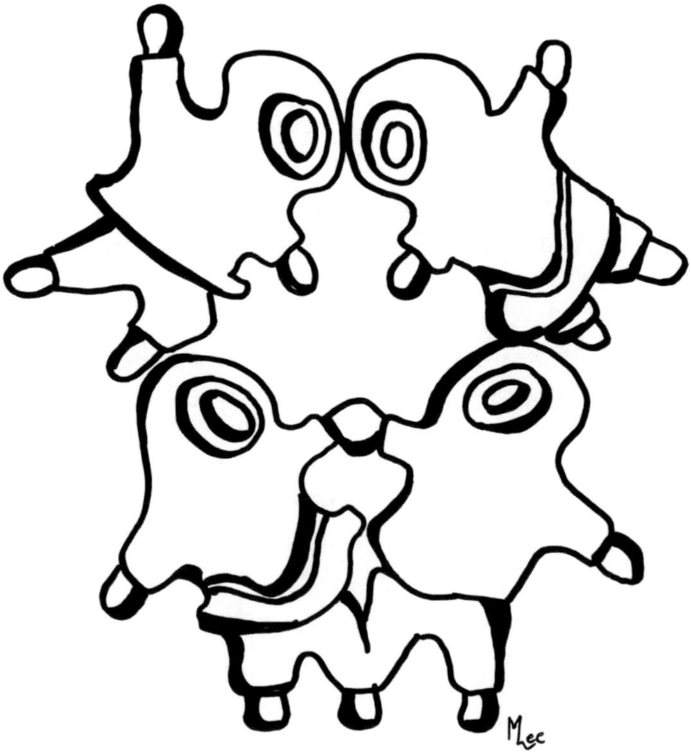
MLee

# Runaway Madness

There is a time in life
when you no longer want the strife
of the day to day trials and tribulation.
What you need is a little soul salvation.
Gather up your things and pack away your sadness,
set your GPS for your runaway madness.

Whatever it is, whatever it requires,
plan your day for your heart's desires.
Peacefulness and talk with friends-
wishing that this time never ends.
Sharing moments of joy and laughter-
not really knowing what comes after.

Knowing for sure there will be consequences-
and realizing you must come to your senses-
you temporarily displace rationalization,
shutting the door to obligation.
For a moment your spirit is free.
You have become the person you want to be.

Runaway madness, runaway madness-
isn't it sad
that things in life can get so bad?
And somewhere in the life you've chosen
you find your spirit and your soul have frozen.
Set yourself free each and every day.
Live not in man's but in Jesus' way.

Diane Lee

MLee

# Rock Idiom

In other times, when grandfathers
and fathers we usually picture
did all the living things
in stages,
orderly sounds were appropriately
beautiful-
like marches or melodies
of popular songs.
Now the mood's grabbed us
in a crashing way,
while the universe
bounces
in its instantly thrilling way.
Metal and stringed parts of us
vibrate within, and now
we surpass the forced square-brown
world.
So we wordlessly smile-
our ears are piqued by joy,
by movement,
and inner drives
shout and sway toward expression.
For once all timed
performance (paid) of necessity
and force dissolve
in better apprehension.
We have our voices back-
restored with simple elevated
chords from forever.
We speak, play, become,
a newly unpredictable sound.
Free.

R.J. Lever

Mee

# The Other Brother

There is one who was never like the rest
in appearance, thought, or action.
In some ways he was the best,
although he never lived up to his own satisfaction.

With words or definitions he never tarried,
always well prepared for the task.
The jobs he chose were always harried,
his talents carefully hidden behind the mask.

Athletic abilities taken in stride,
in trivial pursuit there was none better.
He sometimes worried too much about pride,
and where he stood next to the trendsetter.

The other boys commanded the attention,
although all the same to his mother.
Not aloud did they mention,
he was known as the other brother.

Diane Lee

MLee

# Louie

At the Manor, he was known to all.
The beauty of his puzzles can be seen upon the wall.
In the corner was the gathering place,
for anyone wanting a smile on his face.

Anticipating the return of spring,
we think of the cheer his flowers bring.
At times he struggled for a breath of air,
though his work was completed with a special flair.

He acted unofficially as commander of the boat,
responsible for keeping the spirits afloat.
To all of the weary, he threw out the life buoy.
His name, you may know, is our friend Louie.

Diane Lee

M Lee

# Feelings in Time

In the stillness of a late autumn afternoon,
reflecting on the changing leaves
and the chilled deep blue sky,
I can nearly see a wave
of half-forgotten lovers
moving past.
Within imagined conversations,
I hear mumbled explanations
as eyes meet once again,
after varied paths converge
by coincidence-
compelled to choose
in the intensity of this reverie-
Avert the sadness
or embrace the pain.

R.J. Lever

MLee

# Memories of Love

We sat on a hill in a park
in the springtime
and it was warm and green
and your eyes danced
and I loved you.
Even now, after all the time
and numerous
passing dreams,
I can be there on that hill next to you-
feeling the hopeful
joy of youth,
surrounded by the presence of
You.
The greenness of that hill,
and all the carefree sounds and laughter,
when the coming weight of living
is so distant,
are etched as clearly as
the memory
of you.

R.J. Lever

MLee

## *A Park: Early Evening-the Fall*

***All the beautiful ones glide***

***and seem to say***

***I want to be your love.***

***It's Electric!***

***This primal exchange of light and darkness-***

***It's happened***

***beyond all measure of time.***

***It's now.***

***All the knowing ones***

***glide and seem to say***

***I want to be your***

***Love.***

*R.J. Lever*

M Lee

# Rhonda

Rhonda's in circles
like planets and stars.
Her glance is quite magic
like Venus with Mars.
So Rhonda's the princess,
so fair and so wise,
and Rhonda will work you
like you are the prize.
She'll show you to heaven
on fantasy's wings,
or alternate places
to give you nice things.
But you are a winner because
you've been there.
For Rhonda's the princess,
so wise
and so fair.

R.J. Lever

# Sisters

You know you can count on your sister to be by your side,
even when it can be a difficult ride.
She stands up for you when you don't have the nerve,
and gives you strength when life throws you a big curve.

When all are gone, you still have a friend,
circling around with a helping hand to lend.
Even when she's over her head in trouble,
she envelops you in a protective bubble.

When banded together they accomplish great feats,
and stand proudly when they walk down the streets.
Together with wings their spirits will soar,
and later the sounds of laughter will roar.

Diane Lee

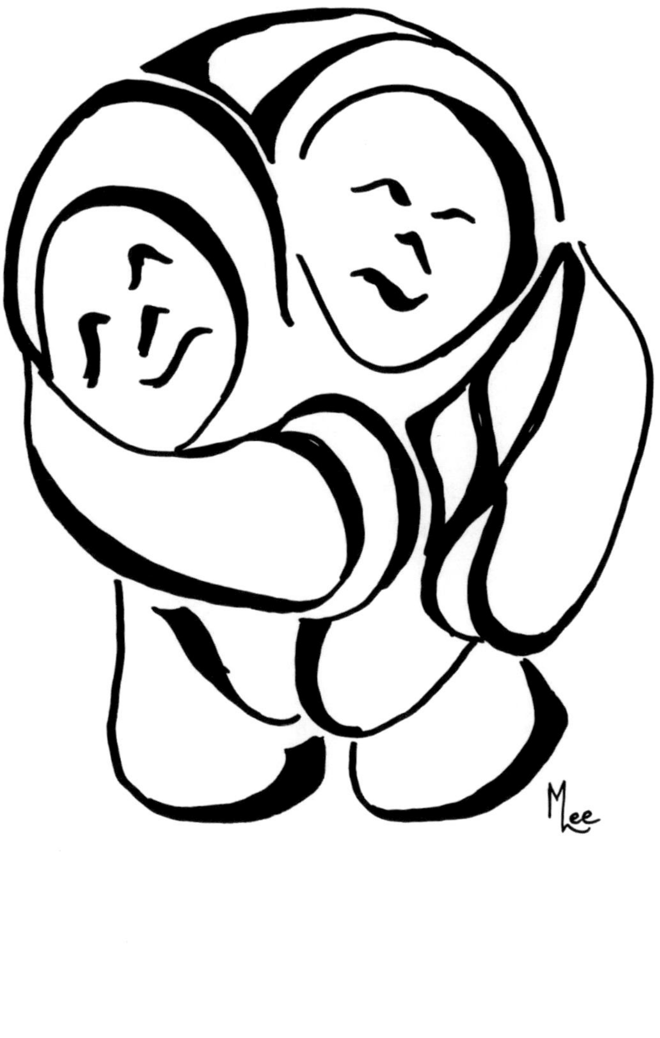
MLee

# Factors of Ten

It’s simple to see and explain
you and me.
Obviously, no one could see all those
Factors of ten.
Who could invent
with all the yearning and strife,
how the processes went with
Factors of ten?
Before us and we,
before twos and three,
Who could foresee all those
Factors of ten?
Chivalry and what has to be,
all must obey
Factors of ten.
And who lost and won,
and wars once begun,
all started once with
Factors of ten.
So let’s find the cause
of loss and of love,
before we embrace
Factors of ten.

R.J. Lever

MLee

# Walking the Fine Line

Gracefully teetering on the line,
we are all so close every day.
There really isn't such a big gap.
Security may be only temporary.

One who takes his meds and one who doesn't-
One who gives and one who receives-
Which one is which is really unknown.
The circumstances may change in an instant.

The very bad have their moments of good;
the good have their moments of bad.
The insane have moments of clarity;
while the "normal" have their lapses.

The direction of the sway is determined by one step.
What drives the step is the concern.
Where's the line and do you see gray?
Or is it meant to be black or white?

Diane Lee

# Jenni's Dream

Jenni is gentle;

Jenni is kind.

She's got a heart that can sing.

Jenni has motion;

Jenni knows things;

Jenni still wants

a life that has wings.

Jenni stands strong;

Jenni can feel;

and Jenni still wants

a life that is real.

R.J. Lever

MLee

# The Plane Ascension

I could not have prepared more, or less,
for the journey of awareness I would take.
Consumed by the eagerness and anticipation
of the dawn of early morning,
in the company of the only one who can mirror my image-
my son,
I thought of the loved ones I would again meet
and the momentary lack of worldly obligation and desire.
As the plane takes off down the runway,
the noise and chatter increase.
Slowly, we ascend to cruising altitude,
leaving all the clutter behind,
and breaking through the clouds until
we are flying at steady state.
Anxiety and fears left behind in a different place,
I am surrounded by the magic of the misty hues
swirling above and through the dreamlike clouds.
I pause to reflect
on the clarity of the nothingness
that coexists with the presence.
The ascension to the realm of the divine has taken place
without warning-
The plane where time and space interconnect.
There is no other awareness,
no past, no future.
I have arrived at my destination,
unknown at the start of my journey.
I am Present
in the joy of the moment!

Diane Lee

MLee

# Song of the Red Desert

Off the path of clock-driven commerce,
where truckers and salesmen
race to achieve documentable results,
lies an expanse-
flatness-
a far-off horizon-
dunes of wind-swept sand-
very few humans-
and silence.
We all keep passing it-
racing by again
as if we've lost
our peripheral vision.
Could we ever stop,
sweep the terrain with our senses,
for once-
begin to see coyotes, foxes,
struggling desert growth?
Could we listen to
the wind-
whatever motion of living
we might chance to hear?
The sunlight, sand, and horizon
speak their own (inimitable) way.
If just one time we were alert to it,
could we arrange to
stop, look, listen-
like Indians, pioneers, and settlers once did?
If we could stop this racing,
this striving,
for two hours, or thirty minutes,
and not measure our living,
could we hear Nature singing-
the desert singing?

R.J.Lever

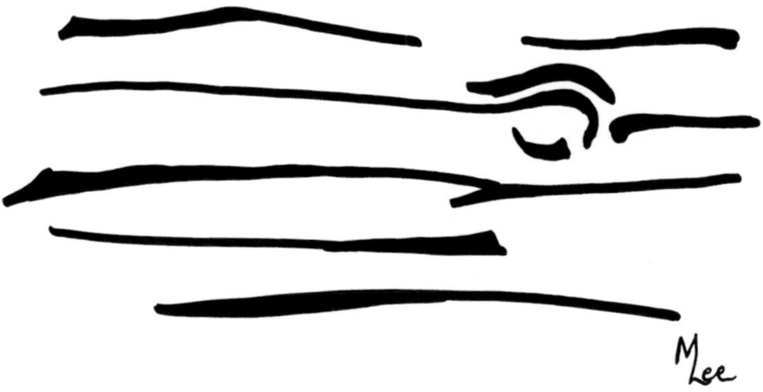
M Lee

# The Quantum Ballet

The artistic melding of energy and light,
creates a dazzling, sparkling, and shimmering sight.
As the sunlight tiptoes on the surface of the water's gentle flow,
it connects to the vision of heaven's wondrous glow.

The senses confused and intertwined,
into one sense they are combined.
There's a symphony of light without sound,
while the visual music plays all around.

Diamonds of light dance as fireflies in flight,
and lead awareness to a greater height.
Moving gracefully and purposely with a wave of flutter,
there's a glimpse of hope through the eyes' open shutter.

Streams of photons beam in a row,
to perform in unison a radiant show.
This harmony of particles that glide and sway,
perfect the evening at the quantum ballet.

Diane Lee

MLee

# Adirondack Sense

It is something that becomes part of you,
no matter where you go:

The smell of Balsam in the air,
triggering a distant memory.

The sight of the glistening cognac colored water,
reflecting a peace and solitude unknown.

The sound of loons over the lake,
echoing a familiar sound.

The feel of a warm rain on the dock,
awakening your vitality.

The taste of sweet maple,
reminding you of your childhood.

It is something that only some possess-
it is the Adirondack Sense.

Diane Lee

MLee

# Balancing Act

The vision of the carefree bear,
sauntering along,
making his passage
from one end of the fallen
and decayed log to the other,
displays more to us
than we have time to understand.
If we paid attention,
we could see where we go wrong.
It appears to be so easy,
one small step after another-
his clumsiness transforming into grace-
focusing on the task instead of being queasy.
He accomplishes with ease
that which appears unlikely
due to his stature.
Perhaps we have utilized
too much consciousness,
looking to ourselves
for all the answers
and
placing too much trust
in human importance
to see
that we have
the innate potential
to perform
a
balancing act
of our
own.

Diane Lee

Mlee

# The Fractured Rock

I recognize the similarity between you and I,
watching as the water swiftly flows by.
There was a time when you also resisted the stresses,
no longer possessing the fortitude or will to try.

A survivor in the river, standing your ground,
while the current travels through and around.
You have adapted and still remain-
the secret of your existence found.

You could have easily lost your position,
submitting to the flow instead of accepting transition.
An individual in the river of life,
holding steady against the competition.

The fractured rock that attracts my gaze,
teaches me clarity through the haze.
It meekly demonstrates the ability to carry on,
with stoic posture and steadfast ways.

Diane Lee

Mee

# Six Mile Run

Pounding along, a while before dusk-
gazing ahead-far off
at the horizon,
suddenly I'm aware of motion
and breath and of
the striving for youth
that's truly gone.
There's a casting off of
numberless (weighty) burdens-
not least of all that
inexorable net of time.
Yet I feel that rare freedom
(that's always been there).
Within this rhythm there's an
escape and peace
that's more than fantasy,
more real than anyone could know.
So, pounding along, I'm one with light,
the greenness of hills, hard earth,
and all the constant rushing of air.
Though moving, I pause to listen for
Nature's own silent song.

R.J. Lever

MLee

# Ode to a Speed Skater

Eagerly awaiting the start of the race,
he anticipates his desired pace.
Slowly positioning himself at the start,
he feels as though he's swallowed his heart.

A seasoned athlete is the one who knows
the feeling when the adrenaline flows.
One of them who is emotionally wired
will begin before the gun is fired.

Back again to the beginning,
soon they will know who is winning.
All is quiet except the tink,
the sound of the skates gliding on the rink.

The fluidity of movement all in tune-
one wrong step can be his ruin.
The ice so glassy, smooth and clear
could not possibly intend to interfere.

Rounding the bend, the end is near,
the crowd begins to stand up and cheer.
He crosses the line and looks up in the light,
the world record posted in his sight.

Skating the victory lap in disbelief,
for a moment the sentiment is relief.
Then he realizes he's reached his goal,
thankful for the resources found deep in his soul.

Diane Lee

MLee

# Christmas Poem:

# The Magi and the Beasts

What did the wise men
know so much better
than the rest?

Was it Aristotle
or how Plato
used to dress?

Had they read the
prophets; could they
speak on their behest?

Were they skilled
in magic? The
constellations of the west?

Or did they make
strange potions, and
had they passed the test?

They surely spied a
star way off
in the east.

They took the
deepest faith
to the humblest
and the least.

And found the Mighty King
in a manger
by the beasts.

R.J. Lever

M Lee

# Discovering Christmas

What do you see and what do you hear on Christmas morn?
Are you aware your Savior is born?
He's born to create a world anew,
perhaps to change what you think and do.

Many rush about with barely a clue.
Many have hearts that are not true.
They frantically accumulate…It's never enough!
They're never at peace…in spite of this stuff.

Christmas is meant to be celebrated each day,
with the light of our Savior guiding our way.
It's for looking into the sky above,
expecting to see a bright star or a dove.

These symbols remind us of a gift to all,
given freely when we hear his call.
Listen to the melody each morning will bring,
you may be surprised at the new song you'll sing.

Christmas is that time of year,
when open hearts and minds can hear.
As sounds of joy and peace abound,
we know our Savior has been found.

This daily gift of our Morning Star,
serves to keep us from drifting afar.
We'll find our direction and know our way,
when we grasp the meaning of Christmas Day!

Diane Lee
R.J. Lever

MLee

# Saturday People:

# Clearer Dreams and Last Refrains

**Saturday people still remember**
**their favorite friends, the best parts of old songs,**
**all their first times,**
**and the thrill of breaking**
**Free.**
**Saturday people just may have**
**occasional notions of starting again;**
**of seeing in a different light;**
**of finding all the better things.**
**Saturday people would probably**
**just smile and nod at you and me.**

**R.J. Lever**

MLee

## About the Authors and Illustrator

***R.J. Lever*** grew up in Clinton New York and graduated from Syracuse University with a degree in Political Science. His affinity for nature and outdoor activities drew him to the West, where he lived in Southwestern Wyoming as well as Colorado Springs Colorado. He worked in the Insurance Business for several years which allowed him to travel along many vast and open expanses. He currently uses these experiences for his creative inspiration and endeavors. He has always been an avid sports fan and continues to participate in activities such as running and hiking. He resides in Central New York and frequents the Adirondacks where he is able to pursue his interest in writing, poetry and nature.

***Diane Lee*** also grew up in Upstate New York in proximity to the Adirondacks, where she developed a love of nature, animals, and active outdoor pursuits such as hiking and distance running. She's a graduate of Clinton Central High, and Ithaca College, completing Ithaca's physical therapy program on the campus of Albert Einstein College of Medicine in the Bronx. She decided to leave the city and chose to relocate to Southwestern Wyoming, where she lived and practiced physical therapy for many years. She now spends time with her family in Wyoming as well as the Adirondacks, where the beauty and diversity of these two regions inspire her creativity and joy in living.

Illustrator and award winning Adirondack Storyteller ***Mitch Lee***, is a Native of Inlet, New York in the Heart of the Adirondack Mountains. His first home was beside the remains of French Louie's Fireplace on Big West Lake. (Now part of the Forever Wild Wilderness Tract known as the West Canada Lakes). Flying in and out of this cabin home with no road by sea plane gave him an early view of the Mountains that inspire him today.

Mitch chooses to find unique ways to make a living in the Adirondacks through caretaking, PR and tourism and as a columnist sharing illustrations and short stories as seen in the *Adirondack Weekly* newspaper. His experiences help to inspire him to weave together the lore and magic of Adirondack traditions through humor, awe and empathy.